ANDRE

Andre, Andre
Is a seal.
He eats fish
For every meal.
For lunch and dinner
That's OK,
But fish for breakfast?
Just — NO WAY!

JAKE

When Jake was at Lake Umbagog,
He felled a tree and made a log.
He fitted logs together, so,
And watched his little cabin grow.
He made a roof and windows tight,
And he slept soundly through the night.

DESERT OF MAINE

I know a place where it's fun to go;
It's the biggest sand pile that you'll ever know.
It covers a house, it covers a plain,
It covers a farm: it's the Desert of Maine.

FIRST STAR

Star light,
Star bright,
First star
I see tonight;
Lead me out
Of stress and strain;
Put me on
The road to Maine.

A STORY

I'll tell you a story
About an old dory,
And now my story's begun.

I'll tell you "anudder",
That it had no rudder,
And now my story is done.

OLD ORCHARD BEACH

I do not see an orchard here;
There's not a single tree.
The pier is near, the beach in reach,
I see the shining sea.

But not an apple do I find,
Nor plum — nor pear — nor peach.
I wonder why they call this place
Old Orchard Beach?

BALD EAGLE

Eagle, eagle, flying high;
I saw you go soaring by.
Did you get bald as you got big?
And do you, sometimes, wear a wig?

BARNACLES

Barnacles cling to rocks and docks.
They cling to ships at sea.
If I stand in the ocean long enough,
Will barnacles cling to me?

THE LIGHTHOUSE

The lighthouse has a single eye
Shining out to sea.
I watched it just the other night.
Guess what? It winked at me.

A WHALE OF A TALE

Four whales swam into the harbor
To see what they could see.
One wandered away in the pea soup fog,
And then there were only three.

Three whales swam into the harbor;
They wished to enjoy the view.
One followed a fisherman out to sea,
And then there were only two.

Two whales swam into the harbor;
They played till the day was done.
One spouted and sprayed in a little cove,
And then there was only one.

One whale swam into the harbor;
Alone, it was not much fun.
So he went looking for other whales;
And then, my friend, there were none.

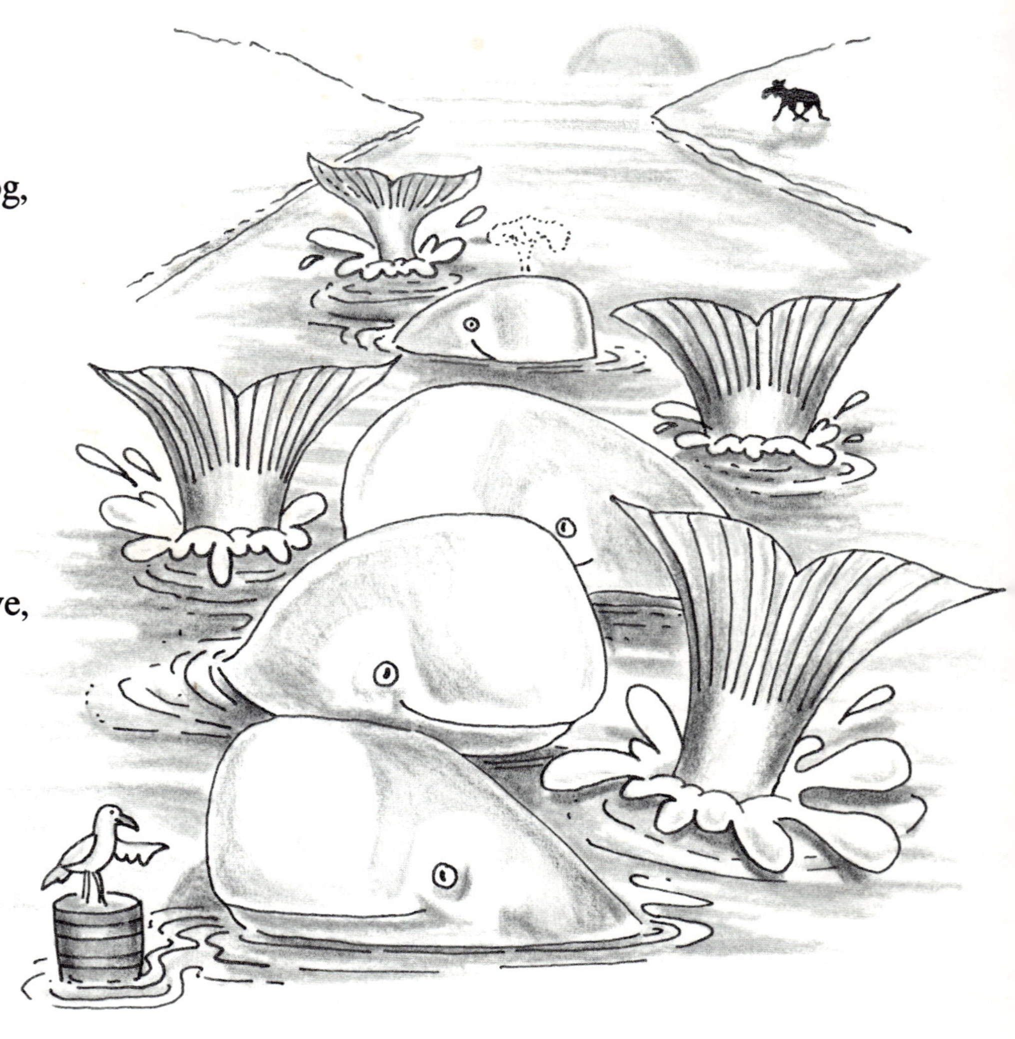

THE STARFISH WISH

When you wish upon a star,
It's not hard to do,
If it happens to be night
And lots of stars shine through.

But if you need to make a wish
In the middle of the day,
Find a starfish at the beach
And this is what you'll say:

Starfish, starfish, swimming free,
Please don't swim away from me.
I wish I might,
I wish I may,
Have the wish I wish today.

PAPOOSE MOOSE

There was hung,
    by a young father moose,
A large bed
    from the top of two spruce.
He explained its great size
With love in his eyes:
"It's to cradle our little papoose!"

KING KATAHDIN

We called on King Katahdin,
Sitting on his granite throne.
His lap was full of fleecy clouds,
And he began to moan.
"To catch these little shavers
Took me almost half the day.
I wish that you had seen the size
Of those that got away!"

A MAINE RIVER

Eastport, Westport,
Northport, South,
Here is the river,
And here is the mouth.
Why does the river
Remain in bed?
Why does the mouth
Run away from the head?

TURTLE

The turtle lives inside his shell.
I guess he likes it rather well.
It goes with him if he should roam,
It's like a mini-motor home.

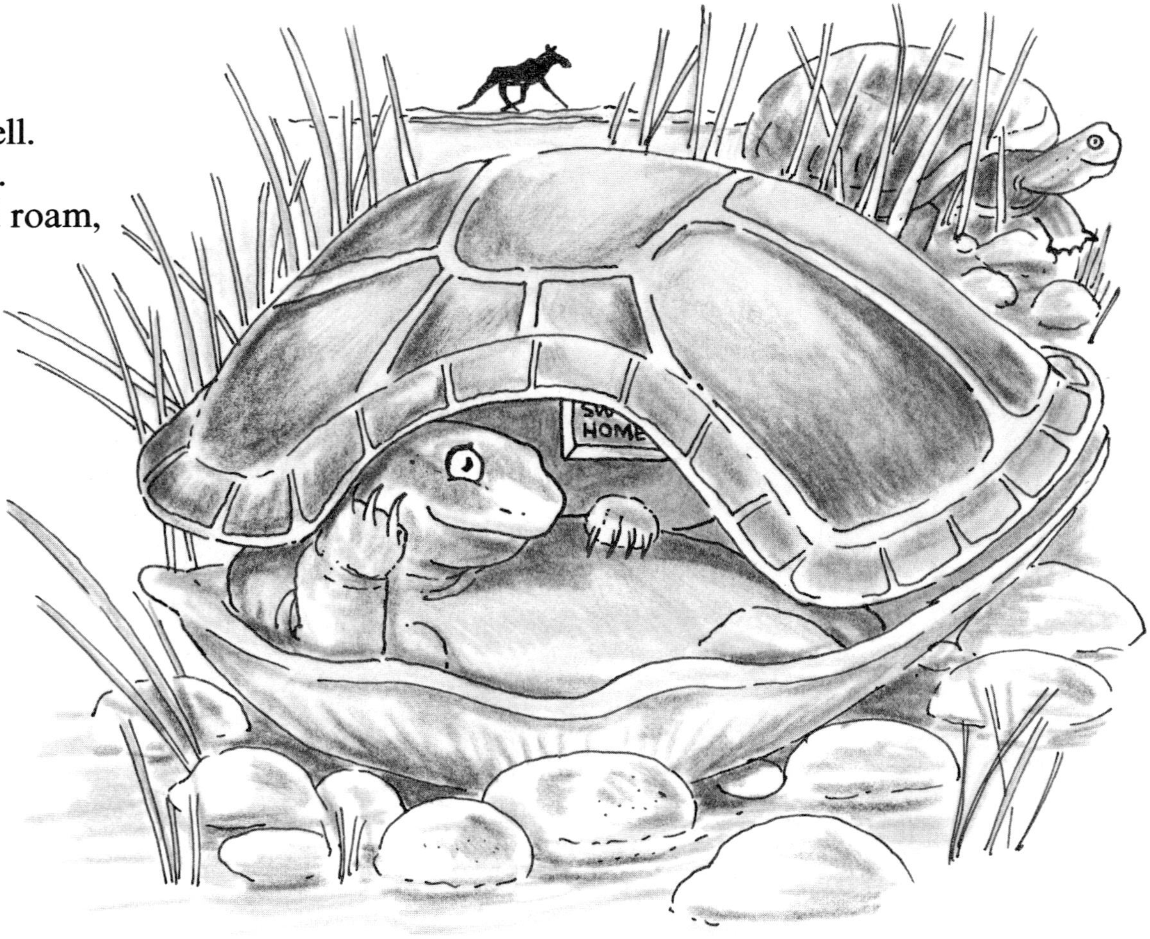

MOUNTAIN COUNTIN'

One, two,
Mt. Blue;
Three, four,
Mt. Dorr;
Five, six,
Mont Dix?
Seven, eight,
Bald Pate;
Nine, ten,
Katahdin!

GOING HIKING

When Mother Moose hikes
Up the mountain track,
She carries Papoose
In her trusty pack.
He can look all about
If that's what he chooses,
Or snuggle inside
For quick little snoozes.
And when they arrive,
At the mountain peak,
Poor Mother is tired
And winded and weak.
But little Papoose
Slides to the ground,
And frolics about
With a leap and a bound.

ACADIA RECIPE

Take one part mountains,
One part ocean, too;
Sprinkle in some islands
So there'll be a view.
Put cliffs along the mountains;
Face them to the east;
Then top it all with forest:
Your eyes will have a feast.

THERE WAS A YOUNG MOTHER

There was a young mother
Lived in a canoe.
Although it was crowded,
She knew what to do.
Some kids were in diapers,
And some were in jeans,
She took them all shopping
At . . . L. L. Bean's.

BLUEBERRIES

Mother Moose, Mother Moose,
What do you make?
Blueberry pie and blueberry cake;
Blueberry jam for blueberry bread,
Blueberry rolls might be good instead;
Blueberry juice, just take a few sips,
And kiss your mother with blueberry lips.

JAM SESSION

Ol' Black Bear had a hankering
For something on her bread.
She was getting very tired
Of that ordinary spread.
She picked berries from the bushes,
And she put them on to stew.
She squished them and she squashed them,
And she stirred in sugar, too.
When she tried some for her lunch,
She was happy as a clam;
For she found she had invented
Maine's great Black Bear-y Jam!

SPELLING LESSON

One goose is a goose;
One moose is a moose.
My tooth is loose.

Two geese are geese;
Are two moose meese?
Are my teeth leese?

RACCOON

Raccoon up an oak tree,
Waiting for the night;
Crawled into our woodshed
By the soft moonlight;
Hungry for his supper,
Eating garbage from a pail;
Along came Jonathan
And grabbed him by the tail.

TRAFFIC JAM

Old Mother Moose
When she wanted to wander,
Would drive into town
In her shiny new Honda.
The traffic was heavy,
Rush hour came on,
She covered her ears
At the strange type of horns.
Once the light turned to green,
Mother Moose was no fool,
She drove to the forest,
So quiet and cool.

JUMP ROPE VERSE

Fanny's gone to Fryeburg
To take in the fair.
What will she see
While she is there?
One roller coaster,
Two tumbling clowns.
Three pulling oxen,
Four quilts of down;
Five jars of marmalade,
Six yearling sheep,
Seven racing sulkies,
Eight babes asleep;
Nine singing cowboys,
Ten balloons, and then
When she has seen it all,
She'll come back home again.

FERRY BOAT

A ferry with a great, blue nose
Lies down Bar Harbor way;
And it sails off to Canada
Nearly every day.
All kinds of people ride her,
The old, young, short, and tall.
Let's watch their cars all drive aboard,
The funniest sight of all.

MAURICE

Blueberry pie and cherry cake,
Maurice went to Moosehead Lake.
What did he see there free and loose?
Not just the head, but the whole live moose!

LOON

See a loon and stay away;
You'll feel happy all the day.
Scare a loon and still its song;
You'll feel sad, the whole day long.

CAMPFIRE

Sing a song of campfires,
Flames aburning bright.
See them lick the corners
Of the deep, dark night.
See them leap up higher;
See the light they make,
Dancing with the moonbeams
On the quiet lake.

POTATOES

Bake 'em,
Flake 'em,
Make 'em into stew.
Chip 'em,
Whip 'em,
Any way will do.

Mash 'em,
Hash 'em,
Give 'em all a chew.
Aroostook potatoes
Have their eyes
On you!

LOBSTER

Some like it hot,
Some like it cold,
Some like it in the shell
(Not too old).
Some like it Newburg,
Some like it stew;
As long as it's lobster
Any way will do!

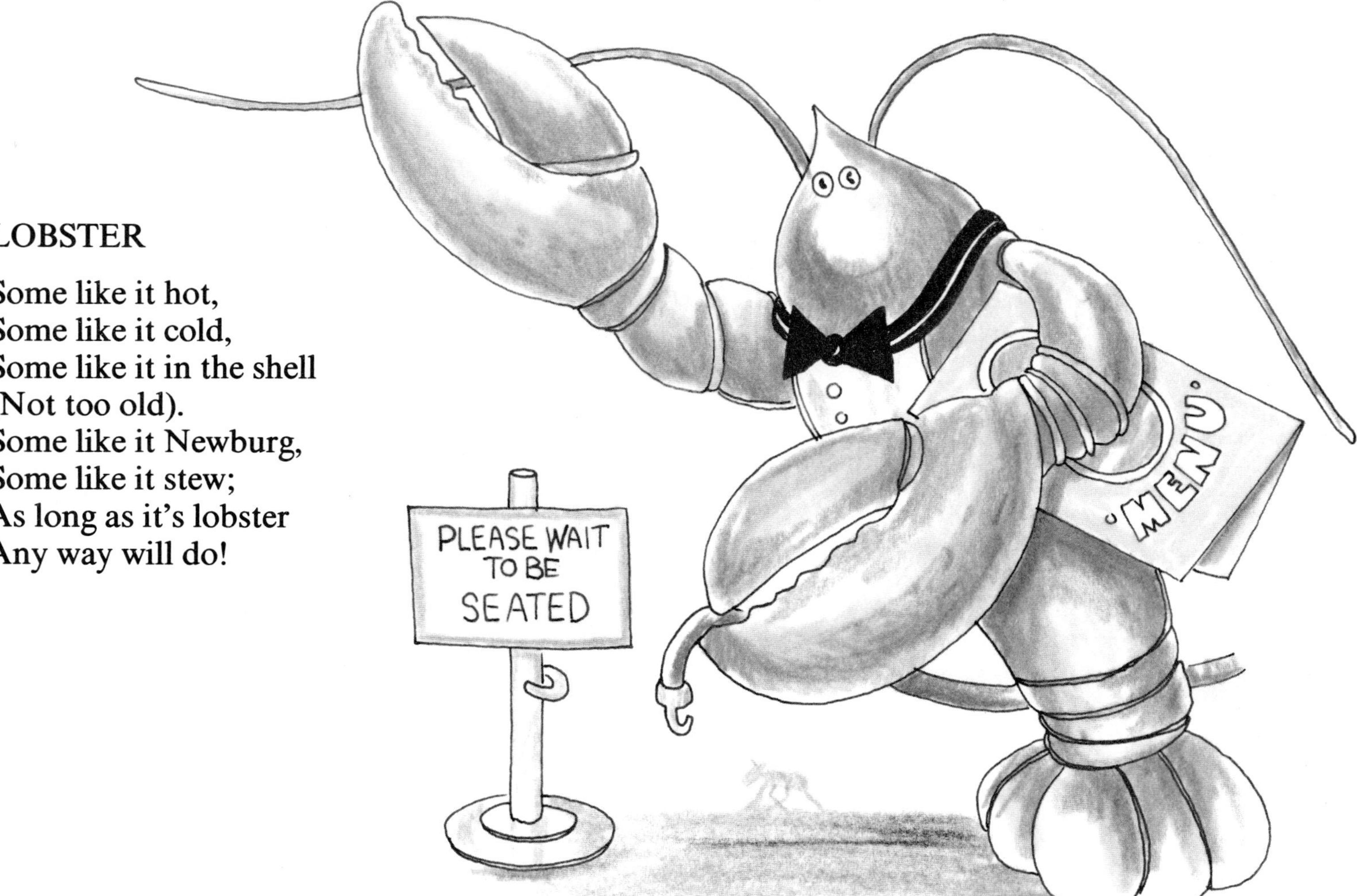

DON'T LEAVE MAINE, WE'VE GOT IT!

China, Denmark, and Peru,
Scotland, Wales, and Mexico, too;
Lisbon, and Lake Norway's shore;
Poland, the Orient, even more;
Stockholm, Sweden (the real McCoy?);
Athens, Carthage, Naples, Troy;
Paris, Frankfort, also Rome:
All in Maine, not far from home!